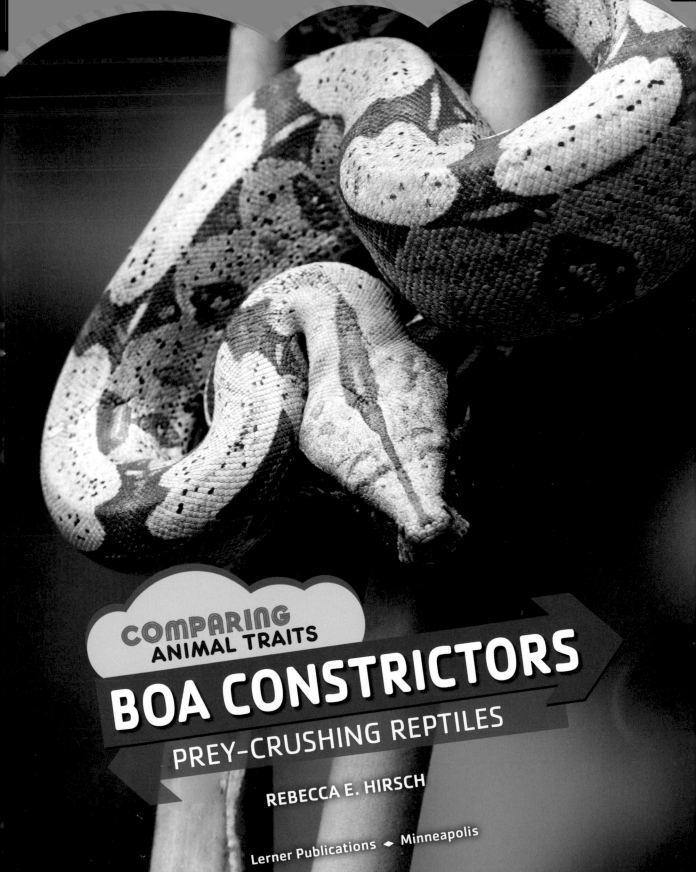

COMPARING
ANIMAL TRAITS

BOA CONSTRICTORS

PREY-CRUSHING REPTILES

REBECCA E. HIRSCH

Lerner Publications ◆ Minneapolis

Lerner Publications Company
A division of Lerner Publishing Group, Inc.
241 First Avenue North
Minneapolis, MN 55401 USA

For reading levels and more information, look up this title at www.lernerbooks.com.

Photo Acknowledgments

The images in this book are used with the permission of: © Michael Lustbader/Science Source/Getty Images, p. 1; © NaturePL/SuperStock, p. 4; © Minden Pictures/SuperStock, pp. 5, 25 (top); © Colombini Medeiros, Fabio/Animals Animals, p. 6; © Zigmund Leszczynski/Animals Animals, pp. 22, 24; © Alkhabazov/ Dreamstime.com, p. 7 (top); Otto Pfister/NHPA/Photoshot/Newscom, p. 7 (bottom); © A & J Visage/Alamy, p. 8; © Fletcher & Baylis/Science Source/Getty Images, p. 9; © iStockphoto.com/cookelma, p. 10; © Paul Whitten/Science Source/Getty Images, p. 11 (bottom left); © iStockphoto.com/richcarey, p. 11 (bottom right); © Laura Westlund/Independent Picture Service, p. 12; © McDonald Wildlife Photography/Animals Animals, pp. 13, 17 (bottom left), 19; © Biosphoto/SuperStock, p. 14; Gerry Ellis/Minden Pictures/Newscom, p. 15; © Doug Wechsler/Animals Animals, p. 16; Jack Goldfarb/Design Pics/Newscom, p. 17 (bottom right); Thomas Marent/Minden Pictures/Newscom, p. 18; © Ameng Wu/iStock/Thinkstock, p. 19 (bottom); © iStockphoto.com/johnandersonphoto, p. 20; © Norbert Probst/imageBROKER/CORBIS, p. 21; © Steve Winter/National Geographic/Getty Images, p. 23 (bottom left); © age fotostock/SuperStock, p. 23 (bottom right); © John Cancalosi/Alamy, p. 25 (bottom); © Auscape/Universal Images Group/Getty Images, p. 26; © iStockphoto.com/bcboy30, p. 27 (bottom left); © Allen Blake Sheldon/Animals Animals, p. 27 (bottom right); © Juergen & Christine Sohns/Animals Animals, p. 28; © Studio Carlo Dani/Animals Animals, p 29 (top); © Paul Starosta/CORBIS, p. 29 (bottom).

Front cover: © Lunatic67/Dreamstime.com.
Back cover: © lunatic67-Fotolia.com.

Main body text set in Calvert MT Std 12/18. Typeface provided by Monotype Typography.

Library of Congress Cataloging-in-Publication Data

Hirsch, Rebecca E., author.
    Boa constrictors : prey-crushing reptiles / Rebecca E. Hirsch.
        pages cm. — (Comparing animal traits)
    Audience: Ages 7–10.
    Audience: Grades K to 3.
    Includes bibliographical references.
    ISBN 978-1-4677-7981-4 (lb : alk. paper) — ISBN 978-1-4677-8276-0 (pb : alk. paper) — ISBN 978-1-4677-8277-7 (eb pdf)
    1. Boa constrictor—Juvenile literature. 2. Boa constrictor—Behavior—Juvenile literature. 3. Boa constrictor—Life cycles—Juvenile literature.
    I. Title.
    QL666.O63H57 2015
    597.96'7—dc23   2014046770

Manufactured in the United States of America
1 – BP – 7/15/15

TABLE OF CONTENTS

MEET THE BOA CONSTRICTOR

A boa constrictor lies coiled on the forest floor. When a rat scurries past, the snake strikes with open jaws. It wraps its body around the rat and slowly squeezes. Boa constrictors belong to a group of animals called reptiles. Other animal groups are mammals, amphibians, birds, fish, and insects.

A boa constrictor squeezes its prey before swallowing it whole.

All reptiles have certain traits in common. Reptiles are vertebrates, animals with backbones. They have scaly skin. Reptiles are cold-blooded and depend on their surroundings to keep their bodies heated. Some reptiles stay warm by living in warm, tropical places. Others lie in the sun to heat their bodies. But boa constrictors also have traits that make them unique.

CHAPTER 1

WHAT DO BOA CONSTRICTORS LOOK LIKE?

Boa constrictors are large snakes with thick, muscular bodies. A boa constrictor can be more than 18 feet (5.4 meters) long. Most are 8 to 13 feet (2.4 to 4 m) long and weigh about 100 pounds (45 kilograms).

Boa constrictors come in different colors and patterns. A boa constrictor's scaly skin can be tan, green, red, or yellow. It may be marked with ovals, diamonds, circles, or zigzag lines. The boa's colors and markings depend on its habitat. The different colors camouflage the boa constrictors in their habitat, helping them disappear into their surroundings.

Dark brown markings help this boa constrictor hide among the leaves.

Boa constrictors have triangle-shaped heads, forked tongues, and dark stripes around their eyes. Their stretchy jaws are lined with many small teeth that curve backward. Boa constrictors use these small, sharp teeth to catch and hold their **prey**. Then they wrap their strong bodies around their captured prey and squeeze until they die from lack of air.

A boa constrictor's tongue is split, ending in two tips.

Boa constrictors have no front legs. Their rear legs are two tiny **spurs**. Each spur looks like a curved claw. Because the spurs are quite small and sit snug against the body, they are difficult to see.

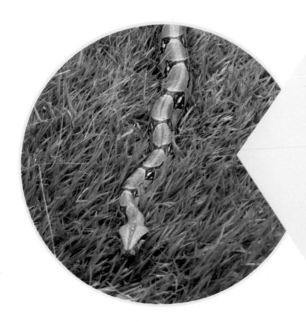

DID YOU KNOW?
Boa constrictors don't **SLITHER** from side to side like some snakes. Instead, they move slowly forward in a straight line.

BOA CONSTRICTORS VS. RETICULATED PYTHONS

Reticulated pythons live in tropical rain forests across Southeast Asia. They are the longest snakes in the world. From head to tail, they can grow nearly 33 feet (10 m) long. That's as long as six grown people lying head to foot! Reticulated pythons may be bigger than boa constrictors, but the two snakes look very similar.

Boa constrictors and reticulated pythons both have long, muscular bodies and patterned skin. A python has gray or tan skin with diamond-shaped markings that act as camouflage. When a reticulated python lies still on the forest floor, its patterned body blends in with the leaves, hiding it from view. Like boa constrictors, reticulated pythons have forked tongues, stripes near their eyes, and tiny rear spurs. Reticulated pythons travel by sliding forward slowly in a straight line.

Reticulated pythons can grow up to 33 feet (10 m) long!

Reticulated pythons look very similar to boa constrictors.

Both boa constrictors and reticulated pythons have bodies well suited for hunting. A python uses its sharp and curved teeth to catch prey, just as a boa constrictor does. The python kills by **wrapping its** muscular body around its prey and squeezing so **tightly that its** prey can't breathe.

BOA CONSTRICTORS VS. HAWKSBILL SEA TURTLES

Hawksbill sea turtles swim near coral reefs around the world. The turtles measure between 2.5 and 3 feet (0.8 to 1 m) long and weigh 100 to 150 pounds (45 to 68 kg). These swimming reptiles look very different from boa constrictors.

Boa constrictors have long, thin bodies. But hawksbill sea turtles have wide, flat bodies covered with thick, bony shells. The carapace, or top shell, is shaped like a shield with a rough edge. The shell is made of large, overlapping scales that are streaked yellow, brown, or orange. The turtle's shell protects the animal from sharks, crocodiles, and other predators. A boa constrictor's body has two tiny back spurs and no front legs. But a hawksbill sea turtle has four flippers with claws. It uses its flippers for swimming.

Hawksbill sea turtles live near coral reefs all around the world.

Boa constrictors have a forked tongue and sharp teeth. Hawksbill sea turtles' tongues are not forked, and the turtles don't have teeth. Instead, hawksbill turtles use their sharp, beaklike jaws for crushing, biting, and tearing soft prey, like sponges and jellyfish.

COMPARE IT!

BOA CONSTRICTORS

VS.

HAWKSBILL SEA TURTLES

8 TO 13 FEET
(2.4 to 4 m)

◄ BODY LENGTH ►

2.5 TO 3 FEET
(0.8 to 1 m)

2 TINY REAR SPURS

◄ LIMBS ►

4 FLIPPERS

Sharp, curved

◄ TEETH ►

None

CHAPTER 2

WHERE DO BOA CONSTRICTORS LIVE?

Boa constrictors live in tropical forests in Mexico and South America. They have adapted to different habitats. You can find boa constrictors in forests, grasslands, deserts, and farm fields. Boa constrictors can sometimes be found in spots near rivers and streams, although they usually stay on land or in trees.

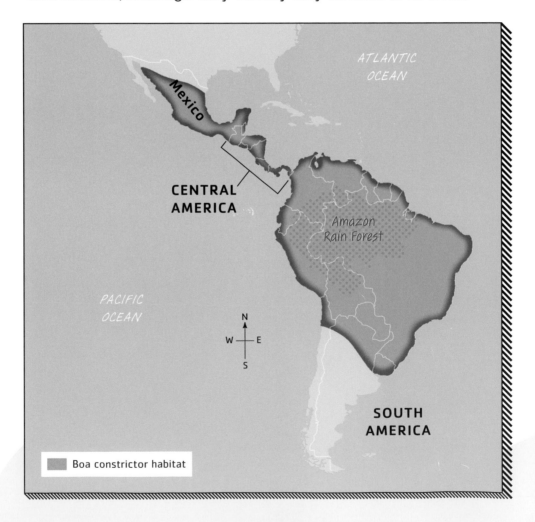

ATLANTIC OCEAN

Mexico

CENTRAL AMERICA

Amazon Rain Forest

PACIFIC OCEAN

N
W—E
S

SOUTH AMERICA

Boa constrictor habitat

Boa constrictors often rest near water.

A boa constrictor's habitat is often the steamy rain forest. Boa constrictors usually stay out of sight, and the forest is filled with good hiding spots. By day, boa constrictors rest in hollow logs, under rocks, and in animals' old **burrows**. Staying hidden protects the boas from predators such as hawks.

At night, boa constrictors coil themselves on tree branches or hide among leaves on the ground. Their patterned skin helps them blend into their surroundings as they wait for prey to come near. Bats are a common meal. Boa constrictors hang from the branches of trees near the mouths of caves and grab flying bats out of the air. Boas also eat birds, rats, squirrels, and frogs. Larger boas dine on bigger prey, like monkeys and wild pigs.

BOA CONSTRICTORS VS. BROWN TREE SNAKES

Brown tree snakes slither through tropical forests in Australia and on islands in the Pacific Ocean. In the past, brown tree snakes lived only in Australia, Indonesia, Papua New Guinea, and the Solomon Islands. But in the last seventy-five years, brown tree snakes were accidentally brought to Guam. The snakes had slithered onto boats or planes heading to the island.

Like boa constrictors, brown tree snakes can live in different habitats. Brown tree snakes are found in forests, grasslands, shrublands, and farm fields. As with boa constrictors, brown tree snakes are often near water. They usually stay on land or in trees.

Similar to boa constrictors, brown tree snakes spend the day sleeping in hidden places such as hollow logs. By night,

DID YOU KNOW?
In movies, boa constrictors are shown as being dangerous to people. In real life, boas are quiet, **CALM** animals and are unlikely to attack a person.

brown tree snakes hunt in the trees or come to the ground to hunt. Like boa constrictors, brown tree snakes eat animals such as birds, lizards, bats, and small mammals. In some parts of the world, brown tree snakes can eat so much prey that they damage their habitat. On the island of Guam, brown tree snakes have caused some birds and lizards to become **extinct**.

BOA CONSTRICTORS VS. NORTHERN WATER SNAKES

A northern water snake swims along the bottom of a pond and snatches a fish in its jaws. Like boa constrictors, northern water snakes are predators, but the two snakes are found in different habitats. Boa constrictors mostly live in tropical habitats in Mexico and South America. Northern water snakes live in the United States and Canada.

Boa constrictors live on the ground and in trees. But northern water snakes live in ponds, lakes, rivers, and marshes. They do sometimes move onto land, but they never go far from the water's edge.

Boa constrictors hunt only at night. But water snakes do most of their hunting during the day. They eat tadpoles, salamanders, frogs, and fish. Water snakes look for prey under logs, near underwater plants, or along the water's edge. Water snakes sometimes use their bodies to catch schools of small fish by trapping them next to a bank. Then the snakes grab them with their jaws.

This northern water snake swims in Maurice River of New Jersey.

COMPARE IT!

BOA CONSTRICTORS

VS.

NORTHERN WATER SNAKES

	HABITAT	
TROPICAL FORESTS, GRASSLANDS, DESERTS, FARM FIELDS		FRESHWATER PONDS, LAKES, RIVERS, MARSHES

	GEOGRAPHIC RANGE	
MEXICO AND SOUTH AMERICA		CENTRAL AND EASTERN UNITED STATES AND CANADA

	MAIN FOOD	
Birds, bats, rats, squirrels, frogs, monkeys, wild pigs		Tadpoles, salamanders, frogs, fish

CHAPTER 3

HUNTING WITH BOA CONSTRICTORS

Boa constrictors are nocturnal, or active at night. Because of this, boas wait until night to go out hunting. A boa constrictor hunts alone, staying still and hidden. To find its prey in the darkness, it senses vibrations in the ground and sound waves in the air. It flicks its tongue to smell the air. It touches its tongue to a special organ in the top of its mouth, called the Jacobson's organ, which senses the smell.

Boa constrictors' tongues help them smell.

Boa constrictors swallow their prey whole.

When a meal is near, a boa constrictor strikes. It grabs the prey with its jaws and holds on tight with its many hooked teeth. The snake quickly winds its strong body around the prey animal. Then the snake slowly squeezes until its prey stops breathing. To eat, a boa constrictor opens its stretchy jaws wide and swallows its food whole, headfirst. It takes about four to six days for a boa to fully digest its meal.

DID YOU KNOW?
Boa constrictors move very **SLOWLY**, only 1 mile (1.6 kilometers) per hour. Boas don't chase their prey, so they don't need to move quickly. But when prey is near, boas strike fast.

BOA CONSTRICTORS VS. AMERICAN CROCODILES

American crocodiles glide through rivers, lakes, lagoons, and swamps as they search for prey. These armored reptiles live in parts of North America and South America. American crocodiles and boa constrictors look very different, but they hunt in similar ways.

Both boa constrictors and American crocodiles hunt at night. Both will eat almost anything they can catch. American crocodiles eat fish, small mammals, birds, crabs, frogs, and turtles.

Both boa constrictors and American crocodiles remain hidden while hunting. An American crocodile waits in the water with only the top of its head exposed. The crocodile can hold its breath for up to an hour, so even its snout can

DID YOU KNOW?
American crocodiles will **SPIT UP** small amounts of food. They use the food as bait to attract fish.

be underwater. Its eyes and ears are on top of its head, so it can look and listen for its prey. And its skin can sense tiny ripples in the water from swimming prey.

As with a boa constrictor, an American crocodile waits for a meal to get close before it strikes. The crocodile grabs its meal with its jaws and drags it underwater until the animal drowns. Unlike boa constrictors, American crocodiles don't swallow prey whole. Instead, they tear the meat to pieces with their jaws.

BOA CONSTRICTORS VS. GREEN IGUANAS

Green iguanas live high in the trees in tropical forests in North America and South America. These spiny-backed lizards grow to an average of 6.5 feet (2 m) long from their noses to the tips of their tails. Green iguanas have very different eating habits than boa constrictors.

Boa constrictors eat meat, but adult green iguanas are **herbivores**. They munch on leaves, flowers, and fruit. Younger iguanas will also dine on insects and spiders.

Boa constrictors are nocturnal. But green iguanas are **diurnal**. That means they move about during the day. Boa constrictors live alone, but green iguanas live in groups. Groups of green iguanas search for food and rest on tree branches in the sun to stay warm. At night, they sleep together in trees. Group living helps protect green iguanas from predators.

Green iguanas often perch in trees.

COMPARE IT!

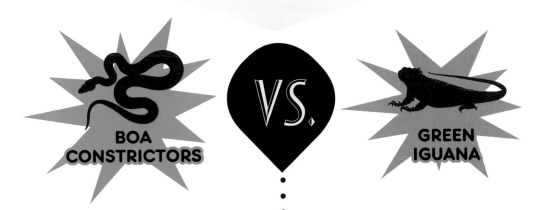

BOA CONSTRICTORS VS. **GREEN IGUANA**

	BEHAVIOR	
LIVES ALONE		LIVES IN GROUPS

	FOOD	
BIRDS, BATS, RATS, SQUIRRELS, FROGS, MONKEYS, WILD PIGS		LEAVES, FLOWERS, FRUIT

	FEEDING TIME	
Night		Day

CHAPTER 4

THE LIFE CYCLE OF BOA CONSTRICTORS

Unlike most reptiles, boa constrictors don't lay eggs. Instead, female boa constrictors give birth to live snakes. After a male and female snake mate, baby snakes grow inside the mother's body. Each growing snake is surrounded by a clear **membrane**. After five to eight months, the mother gives birth to ten to sixty live young. She pushes them out through an opening in her body called the cloaca.

Boa constrictors give birth to live young.

A group of newborn boa constrictors is called a bed.

Each baby boa constrictor can be up to 20 inches (51 centimeters) long. They look like small versions of the adults. They have **inherited** traits, such as the color and the pattern of their skin. When they are born, baby snakes already know how to find food and protect themselves from predators. In two or three years, the snakes are big enough to mate and have offspring of their own. Boa constrictors may survive for twenty to thirty years in the wild.

DID YOU KNOW?
As boa constrictors grow bigger, they **SHED** their skin. The skin splits over the snout and peels back from the body, uncovering a new layer of skin.

BOA CONSTRICTORS VS. BLUE-TONGUED SKINKS

A blue-tongued skink peeks out of a hollow log. This shy lizard lives in Australia, Tasmania, and New Guinea. If disturbed, it hisses loudly and sticks out its bright blue tongue. Blue-tongued skinks and boa constrictors have different behaviors, but their life cycles are similar.

As with boa constrictors, young blue-tongued skinks grow inside their mother's body. About three to four months after mating, the mother gives birth to ten to twenty-five live young. Each baby skink is about 5 inches (13 cm) long and weighs about half an ounce (15 grams).

Newborn blue-tongued skinks know by instinct how to take care of themselves, just like boa constrictors. However, blue-tongued skinks reach adulthood in about a year, much faster than boa constrictors do. Blue-tongued skinks live for twenty years or more, which is almost as long as boa constrictors.

Blue-tongued skinks are named for their large, blue tongues.

COMPARE IT!

BOA CONSTRICTORS

VS.

BLUE-TONGUED SKINKS

LIVE BIRTH	◄ TYPE OF BIRTH ►	**LIVE BIRTH**
2-3 YEARS	◄ REACHES ADULTHOOD ►	**1 YEAR**

20-30 YEARS ◄ LIFE SPAN ► **20 YEARS**

BOA CONSTRICTORS VS. MALAGASY CHAMELEONS

Malagasy chameleons climb trees in forests in Madagascar. These brightly colored reptiles are about 3 to 5 inches (7.6 to 13 cm) long. Their life cycles are very different from those of boa constrictors.

Unlike female boa constrictors, female Malagasy chameleons lay eggs. After a male and female chameleon mate, the female digs a hole in the sand and lays her eggs. The eggs rest in the sand for about eight months.

After the eggs hatch, the baby Malagasy chameleons crawl out of the sand. Each newborn chameleon is about 1 inch (2.5 cm) long. They may be small, but they grow up very fast. Boa constrictors take two to three years to become adults, but Malagasy chameleons reach adulthood in only two months. Then it's time for the adult chamelons to mate. Once they mate,

Malagasy chameleons use their tongues to catch food, including insects.

This Malagasy chameleon clings to a branch.

adult chameleons live for only two or three more months. They do not live to see their eggs hatch nine months later. The entire life span of a Malagasy chameleon, including time inside the egg, is only one year, much shorter than the life span of boa constrictors.

DID YOU KNOW?
Malagasy chameleons live only four or five months after hatching. They have the **SHORTEST** life span of any known four-legged animal.

BOA CONSTRICTOR TRAIT CHART

This book explored the ways boa constrictors are similar to and different from other reptiles. What other reptiles would you like to learn about?

	COLD-BLOODED	SCALES ON BODY	LAY EGGS	SMALL, CURVED TEETH	LIVE IN TROPICAL RAIN FORESTS	ACTIVE MOSTLY AT NIGHT
BOA CONSTRICTOR	X	X		X	X	X
RETICULATED PYTHON	X	X	X	X	X	X
HAWKSBILL SEA TURTLE	X	X	X			
BROWN TREE SNAKE	X	X	X	X	X	X
NORTHERN WATER SNAKE	X	X		X		
AMERICAN CROCODILE	X	X	X		X	X
GREEN IGUANA	X	X	X		X	
BLUE-TONGUED SKINK	X	X				
MALAGASY CHAMELEONS	X	X	X		X	

GLOSSARY

adapted: to have changed over a long period of time to become suited to a particular environment

burrows: holes in the ground made by animals for shelter or protection

camouflage: the hiding or disguising of an animal by covering it up or changing the way it looks

carapace: the upper shell of a turtle

coral reefs: underwater rocky ridges made up of corals, other living substances, and limestone

diurnal: active mainly during the daytime

extinct: when a type of animal no longer exists

habitat: an environment where an animal naturally lives. A habitat is the place where an animal can find food, water, air, shelter, and a place to raise its young.

herbivores: plant-eating animals

inherited: passed on from an animal's parents to their children

instinct: a behavior that is passed on by an animal's parents and is automatic rather than learned

membrane: a thin, soft, flexible sheet or layer

nocturnal: active at night

predators: animals that hunt other animals

prey: an animal that is hunted and killed by another animal for food

spurs: small, stiff, pointed body parts

traits: features that are passed on from parents to children. Body size and skin color are examples of traits.

LERNER

SOURCE

Expand learning beyond the printed book. Download free, complementary educational resources for this book from our website, www.lerneresource.com.

SELECTED BIBLIOGRAPHY

Areste, Manuel, and Rafael Cebrian. *Snakes of the World.* New York: Sterling, 2003.

"Boa Constrictor." Maryland Zoo. Accessed November 1, 2014. http://www.marylandzoo.org/animals-conservation/reptiles/boa-constrictor/.

Lindemann, Laurel. "Boa Constrictor." *Animal Diversity Web.* Accessed October 31, 2014. http://animaldiversity.ummz.umich.edu/accounts/Boa_constrictor/.

O'Shea, Mark, and Tim Halliday. *Reptiles and Amphibians.* New York: Dorling Kindersley, 2002.

Tyning, Thomas F. *Stokes Guide to Amphibians and Reptiles.* Boston: Little, Brown, 1990.

FURTHER INFORMATION

National Geographic: Boa Constrictors
http://animals.nationalgeographic.com/animals/reptiles/boa-constrictor
Discover more interesting facts about boa constrictors. Explore beautiful photos and a habitat map.

San Diego Zoo Animals: Boa
http://animals.sandiegozoo.org/animals/boa
Read about the habitats, the hunting style, and the diet of the boa constrictor and other members of the boa family of snakes.

Wojahn, Donald, and Rebecca Hogue Wojahn. *A Rain Forest Food Chain: A Who-Eats-What Adventure in South America.* Minneapolis: Lerner Publications, 2009. Learn more about the food chains in South American rain forests.

Woodward, John. *Everything You Need to Know about Snakes and Other Scaly Reptiles.* New York: DK, 2013. Explore the world of snakes and other fascinating reptiles in this book.

INDEX